Copyright © 2018 Cherrymoon Media
All rights reserved.
www.cherrymoonmedia.com

ISBN-13: 978-0-9982190-4-2

FOUR VITAL QUES TIONS

FOR TEACHERS AND PRINCIPALS

By Keen Babbage, Ed. D.

CONTENTS

INTRODUCTION

When people in positions of authority or influence in this country are asked how a problem could be solved, often part of the answer is "education." If the issue is a health concern, part of the solution is said to be educating people about the causes of the problem and the ways to prevent encountering it. This nation expects much from education, whether experienced in school or in other ways.

If the issue is related to the economy, part of the answer could be about education which trains people to do jobs which are not being filled today or for which a future need is anticipated. Again, our society relies significantly on education as a process for solving problems and creating opportunities.

When the issue is related to the quality of government or to citizen involvement in political activities, one aspect of the answer is to educate the voters so they can cast informed votes and are aware of ways to be involved in the political process.

If the issue is the quality and the effectiveness of education itself at the elementary school, middle school, and high school levels, people in positions of authority or influence often suggest that more professional development or more continuing education for educators would be beneficial.

There is some merit to those claims for more education in confronting issues and solving problems. In the field of education, the people who know the most about what is occurring and what needs to occur in schools are the people who work at a school all day, every day. Should they continue to learn about their profession? Yes, of course. Are they in a unique position to offer essential and realistic perspectives on schools? Absolutely yes.

This book is designed for teachers and for school principals. This book is designed to be a catalyst for thinking about what matters most and what works best at a school. The reader of this book is asked to become the co-author of the book. As you read this book and write your responses to the questions in this book, please think, think more, keep thinking, and please write, write more, keep writing. When it comes to education, your knowledge of what matters most and what works best is unsurpassed.

There are people who work at schools who are not teachers and who are not principals. Or are they, just in a different and additionally essential way? If you work at a school, you may not be a full-time teacher who is in the classroom all day, and you may not be a full-time school administrator who leads and manages all day, but you can enhance what happens at school.

The teacher category primarily includes educators who are in the classroom with students all day; however, school counselors, school social workers, librarians, and educators with other titles who also work with students are part of the overall teaching process and experience at school. In this book, when the term teacher is used, the reference is in particular to classroom teachers, yet is also designed to include the other educators at a school who work with students and who contribute to the overall instructional work at school.

The principal category includes educators who are the singular administrative leader of a school, yet also includes people in positions such as assistant principal, dean of students, academic dean, instructional coach, and educators with other managerial or leadership titles. Certainly these people work with students and can impact instruction, but their primary duty often is in the leadership and managerial aspects of the school.

The members of the support staff at a school also play important roles which help a school function at its best. Support staff members also can provide helpful insights which should be sought and valued.

People who work in a school district's central office or in a state's department of education have important supportive and managerial duties that are necessary for schools to function well and for education to happen effectively. Whether those people once were a teacher or a school principal or not, they are invited into this book's examination of four vital questions to see how the partnership between their work, those questions, and the people who work in schools can function most productively.

There are many people who seek to impact elementary schools, middle schools, and high schools. These include university and college professors of education, interest groups, political parties, elected officials, community groups, think tanks, charitable foundations, media, and others. With rare exception, these people do not work at a school and may not get to spend much time in schools; nonetheless, they have ideas and concerns. They are encouraged to spend more time in schools so they can hear from the people who work at schools, because those educators who work in schools have the most realistic and current information. They are also encouraged to think about these four vital questions and to talk with educators about the ideas which are prompted by these four vital questions.

Of course, there are more than four questions which can be and should be considered by teachers and principals. The four questions in this book are presented as vital because they are foundational, fundamental, basic, essential, imperative, and integral. As the reader thinks about and writes about the four vital questions, additional questions will come to mind. Please write those questions in this book which you are the co-author of, and give those questions which you create some serious thought. Keep this book and re-read it occasionally to give yourself additional opportunities to reflect, to think, to write, to learn, and to grow in your career.

My career in education includes, thus far, 34 years as a middle school teacher, a middle school administrator, a high school teacher, and a graduate school adjunct instructor. During those years, it has become quite apparent that education is more important than ever, that schools are asked to do more than ever, and that education work is more demanding than ever.

Working in education in general, and working at a school especially, is exhausting and fascinating, inspiring and sometimes heart-breaking, challenging and important, and includes many possibilities to truly make a difference for good in the lives of students. With those realities and ideals in mind, we begin our consideration of Four Vital Questions for Teachers and Principals.

-Keen Babbage, Ed. D.
Lexington, Kentucky
2018

WHAT IS OUR SCHOOL'S MOST IMPORTANT GOAL?

"Our school has many goals. We have a very broad and inspiring mission statement. We have annual performance evaluations for the overall school and for each person who works here. Those evaluations include a long list of specific objectives that get measured. All of our goals and all of our objectives are important. I need to think a lot before I could select the school's most important goal."

Great idea: think a lot. This book is designed to be a catalyst for thinking. The reader of this book is the co-author of this book. Your thoughts will fill many pages of this book. As you read this book, and in times to come whenever you re-read this book, including your writing in this book, you will give yourself an opportunity to think anew, to learn more, to confirm or revise priorities, and to grow both professionally and personally.

What is the school's most important goal? Consider this approach to that question: what goal for your school, when fully reached, will be most beneficial for the largest number of people? You may identify a goal which can be reached only when everyone at the school benefits individually. You may identify a specific goal which is essential for your school to resolve even if it is an issue which directly impacts a portion of the people at the school, but which is urgent because of the overall good it can do for the entire school.

Please keep this in mind: some organizations establish a very long list of goals and the people there must spend endless time seeking to reach all of those goals, while also monitoring their progress or lack of progress toward those goals. That long list of goals may actually be a problem. A long list made up of goal after goal can create much frustration, as no goal is fully reached due to so many goals being pursued.

Instead of causing a possibility of being unsuccessful in the attempt to do everything that can be considered, concentrating on reaching one absolutely vital goal could be more important than the sum of seeking to reach many other goals. Set the right goal. Set the goal that transcends all other goals. Concentrate on the goal that, when reached, has most significantly helped fulfill the purpose of the organization.

Keep in mind that one overall goal may have many steps in the process of reaching that goal. Also, one overall goal may have sub-goals which need to be reached for the overall goal to be reached. The intention is to do the possible rather than to waste time and effort chasing the impossible, the bureaucratic, the unnecessary, or the unnecessarily complex and complicated. Establish the most important goal, then do what matters most and what works best to reach that goal. The results can be truly magnificent, majestic, meaningful, and life-changing.

"One goal? Just one? Schools are asked to do more and more every year. Elementary schools are supposed to somehow make

sure that students are ready for kindergarten, or to compensate for that if the students were not ready. All schools are told to be sure that each student is reading at grade level. Middle schools are directed to address all academic needs of students, while also helping students adjust to the new experiences of being adolescents. High schools must ensure that all students are college-ready or career-ready.

Then each year we get these reforms or innovations or mandates that have to be implemented. Most of these don't work, but we have to go to the training, and we have to do our part to implement them. One goal I have is for the people who make decisions about schools to actually come spend time in schools, work at a school, and listen to people who work at schools before they make their decisions telling us what to do and how to do it. That rarely happens, but I can dream, can't I?

OK. I can do this. One goal that is most important. It makes me think of what I do on New Year's Eve each year. I don't create a long list of resolutions for the year. I think of the one really major change I need to make or the one most consequential improvement I need to make. I concentrate on that and I do much better than if I had a long list which would never get done. Sometimes I add a few changes and improvements as the year goes along, but I really concentrate on the one goal that I decide can do me more good than anything else would. OK, I can do that about our school. What do I think is our school's most important goal?"

Our school's most important goal is...

———

Some reasons why this is our school's most important goal...

———

1.

2.

3.

4.

How will people benefit as we pursue this goal?
———

1.

2.

3.

4.

How will people benefit when we reach this goal?

1.

2.

3.

4.

What are the obstacles our school faces in reaching this goal?

———

1.

2.

3.

4.

What actions are we taking at our school to
overcome those obstacles?

———

1.

2.

3.

4.

What actions am I taking to help our school reach this goal?

—————

1.

2.

3.

4.

How does working toward this goal impact my teaching, my interactions with students, my work with colleagues, the lesson plans I create, the homework I assign, the tests and quizzes I develop, and the way I manage time throughout each day?

———

1.

2.

3.

4.

How does working toward this goal impact the decisions which are made, the priorities which are set, and how time and other resources are used at the school?

———

1.

2.

3.

4.

How does working toward this goal impact the
actions of people who work at the school, but who
are not classroom teachers?

———

1.

2.

3.

4.

*What else could we do each day to move our school
closer to this goal?*

———

1.

2.

3.

4.

What actions do we avoid, not permit, and never allow because those actions would undermine our dedication to and our work toward the goal?

———

1.

2.

3.

4.

How will we know when our school has reached this goal?

_____

1.

2.

3.

4.

What will it mean for and to the following people when our school reaches the most important goal?

———

1. Students at our school

2. Parents and guardians of students who attend our school

3. Teachers who work at our school

4. Principals and other school administrators who work at our school

5. School counselors and librarians who work at our school

6. Support staff who work at our school

7. People who work in our school district's central office

8. Our community, including taxpayers

9. People who work in our state's department of education

10. People who make laws, policies, and regulations about education in our state and in our school district

"But there are so many other goals which we have to work on. Our school district and our state both have these separate, massive documents we have to complete every year showing what our objectives are for the next school year. We have to explain how we are going to reach each of those objectives. We have to tell how we are going to measure progress, and we have to give a mid-year report. All of that takes a lot of time, but it also can seem overwhelming. There are so many goals and so many objectives. What we supposed to do?

I really believe that what I wrote about our school's most important goal is, in fact, the most important goal. But there is so much more we have to do. How is all of that done?"

That is a very realistic question. Think about those other goals and objectives. Select three additional goals, beyond the one you chose as most important, which you decide are ranked second, third, and fourth in terms of importance.

———

2.

3.

4.

Now, it is time to think about those additional goals. Check to see if the additional goals you wrote are consistent with the goal that you decided is the most important goal for your school. There should be complete compatibility. There should be no contradictions. Ideally, the additional goals you wrote would be supportive of and would be steps toward or parts of reaching the most important goal.

Here is what is similar across the four goals I have written...

_____

1.

2.

3.

4.

Here is what is different across those goals as I look at them...

———

1.

2.

3.

4.

Let's further reflect upon a point made earlier: it is possible that a school is better served with a single-minded concentration on one magnificent goal which pursues the most important result that could be obtained. When a school is required to set too many goals, the efforts to reach all of the many goals can be so divided that no goal is reached. What do you think about that idea of concentrating on the one most important goal?

Here's what I think...

_____

As you think about the most important goal for your school, it is a good time to think about the goals you initially set for yourself when you became an educator. Perhaps you were inspired by a strong sense of making the world a better place by providing outstanding educational experiences for students. You may be related to people who had worked in schools, and you saw in their career experiences something that you sought for yourself.

You have been thinking about the most important goal for your school, but before we leave the topic of that most important goal, let's take some time for each reader to personalize this approach. What goals have been most important to you during your career, and what goal is most important to you in your career now?

When I decided to become a teacher, my most important goal was...

———

During the years of my teaching career, at various times I have had these additional goals...

———

1.

2.

3.

4.

Right now, my most important goal in my teaching career is...

———

When I left classroom teaching and became a principal, an assistant principal, a school counselor, a librarian, an academic dean, a dean of students, an instructional coach or other position at a school, my most important goal was...

———

During the years since I left classroom teaching and have done other work in a school, I have had these additional goals...

—————

1.

2.

3.

4.

In my work now at school as a principal or other educator with leadership and management duties, my most important goal in my education career is...

———

Let's put all of this together. You have identified and thought about the most important goal for your school. You have reflected upon professional goals you had when you selected education as your career and that you have had throughout your career. The topic to ponder is whether everything is symbiotic.

The ideal would be for the most important goal for your school to be one which works very cooperatively with the most important goal you have for your career. That would mean the school is reaching its most important goal as you are reaching your most important career goal. The work you do to reach your career goal helps the school reach its most important goal. When pursuit of and fulfillment of the most important goal for the school is enhanced through the pursuit of and the fulfillment of your most important career goal, everyone wins and the beneficial results multiply.

Consider a school which has clearly identified its most important goal for the current school year. At this school, every person who works at the school has identified a goal for himself or herself which is what will be achieved for professional growth this year and which is supportive of the school's most important goal. When the individual goals are compatible with, complementary with, and united with the school's most important goal, the results for the school as an organization and for everyone at the school—students and employees—can be inspiring, rewarding, meaningful, purposeful, and very worthwhile.

Bring all of the thinking you have done during our chapter one work with you as we explore the topic of chapter two: "Do I always do what matters most and what works best?"

DO I ALWAYS DO WHAT MATTERS
MOST AND WORKS BEST?

An optimistic reformer would say that education is a perpetual pursuit of the perfect process which will guarantee complete academic success for each student. A pessimist, or perhaps the voice of experience, would say that education reforms, innovations, and changes are usually unproductive; often inefficient; rarely worth the time, effort, and money invested in them; limited in what good, if any, they do; and interfere with the real work that needs to be done.

The debate on education reform has a long history. That debate will continue, as will education reform efforts. Individual educators have a professional and contractual obligation to comply with laws, regulations, policies, and directives. Those mandates must be obeyed, but implementing those mandates is part, not all, of the work which conscientious teachers, principals, assistant principals, deans of students, academic deans, school counselors, instructional coaches, and librarians do.

Even with mandates that are imposed on schools, educators have two options: complain constantly or implement conscientiously, getting any good results which are possible from each mandate.

There is a third factor which goes beyond those two options.

The third factor is what else you do in addition to the mandates and how you do that additional work. Do not let the bureaucratic mandates define you as an educator. Instead, be defined as an educator who always does what matters most and who always does what works best.

In what ways can we identify what matters most and what works best? Start with this, please: think of the best teacher you ever had. Mentally put yourself back into the classroom of this superior teacher. What did that teacher do which earns for him or her the evaluation of being the best teacher you have had during all of your years as a student?

You are able to clearly and vividly identify what your best teacher did. Make a list of what that teacher did, and you will be on your way toward identifying what matters most and what works best.

1.

2.

3.

4.

Because of what your best teacher did, there emerges an understanding of what mattered most about education to that teacher. Reflect again about your best teacher, and this time identify what that teacher's actions reveal about what mattered most about education to that teacher.

1.

2.

3.

4.

During your career as a student and during your career as an educator, you have known many people who were working in a school, but who were not a teacher. Think of the most exemplary educator whom you have known in one of the following categories: principal, assistant principal, dean of students, academic dean, school counselor, instructional coach, librarian, or other educators who work at a school but who have a different title. What did that person do which causes you to put them at the top of the list of exemplary educators?

1.

2.

3.

4.

Because of what that principal or other educator did, there emerges an understanding of what mattered most about education to that person. Reflect again about that outstanding educator, and this time identify what that educator's actions reveal about what mattered most about education to him or her.

1.

2.

3.

4.

There are standards which must be followed. Anything which can be called what matters most and what works best must be G-rated, legal, ethical, professional, wholesome and beneficial. Laws, regulations, policies, and contractual requirements must be abided by.

Realistic evidence is also a good guide. What are the instructional activities in your classroom that cause the most learning and the best learning? What have you learned from these successes? What instructional activities have you used which did not work? What have you learned from these experiences. Give those questions some thought.

What are the instructional activities in my classroom which cause the most learning and the best learning?

———

1.

2.

3.

4.

What instructional activities have I used which did not work?

1.

2.

3.

4.

What have I learned about teaching and about learning from the instructional activities which were most effective?

———

1.

2.

3.

4.

What have I learned about teaching and about learning from the instructional activities which were least effective?

1.

2.

3.

4.

In my experiences as an educator, what leadership, management, and/or instructional activities have I been involved in or seen which got the best results?

_____

1.

2.

3.

4.

In my experiences as an educator, what leadership, management, and/or instructional activities have I been involved in or seen which did not work?

———

1.

2.

3.

4.

What have I learned about leadership,
management, and/or instruction from the
activities which were the most effective?

———

1.

2.

3.

4.

What have I learned about leadership,
management, and/or instruction from the
activities which were least effective?

———

1.

2.

3.

4.

This time, approach the topics of what matters most and what works best from the perspective of the events of a typical day at school.

List nine very common events on a very usual day at school—from taking attendance to teaching a complex concept, from supervising in the cafeteria to disciplining a student who has repeatedly violated school rules, from counseling a student to coaching a teacher on instructional techniques—and then be ready to evaluate how those events are being done according to what works best and what matters most.

The common events	Are they done in the way which works best?	Are they what matters most?
1.		
2.		
3.		

The common events	Are they done in the way which works best?	Are they what matters most?
4.		
5.		
6.		

The common events	Are they done in the way which works best?	Are they what matters most?
7.		
8.		
9.		

Some of those common events may seem to be procedural, such as taking attendance. Yet, can taking attendance be done in a way which enhances learning? Could each student be asked a short-answer question about work which was done recently in class to refresh the memory instead of merely being asked to reply with "here?" Taking attendance matters and needs to be done. Taking attendance in a way which enhances learning and which begins today's instruction makes attendance taking matter more and puts attendance taking in the realm of being done in a way that works best to help support what matters most.

Thinking in terms of the opposite perspective can be revealing. The opposite of what works best is what does not work at all. Think of some actions you have taken during your career in education which simply did not work. List three of those actions, tell why each failed, and tell what can be learned.

Action taken	Why it failed	What can be learned from those failures?
1.		
2.		
3.		

Is there a common thread among all three of the failures, or did each action fail for a unique reason? If there is a common thread, what is it?

Could the failures be corrected so that based on what did not work, changes can be made and the modified action can work?

The opposite of what matters most is what does not matter at all. The almost opposite of what matters most is what barely matters. Think of ways that time, effort, money, and other resources are used at school for actions which do not matter at all or which barely matter.

What comes to mind?

_____

1.

2.

3.

4.

Why are these actions which do not or barely matter done?

———

1.

2.

Some of those actions which do not or barely matter may be imposed on a school by officials who are in the education hierarchy or who are from an outside group which convinced a school district or a state government to impose some mandate on schools. The people in the hierarchy need to know that some actions they have imposed, even with the best of intentions, did not work, were a poor use of resources, were distractions from what does work, and must not be repeated.

Professionally, politely, and effectively, what could I say to people in positions of authority which could help them realize that schools need to do only what matters most and only what works best?

———

Think about a full day at school. How do you use your time? Do you teach classes throughout the full day? Do you have some time to plan lessons or to prepare instructional materials? Are you in meetings much of the day? Do you counsel students during part of the day or during much of the day? Do you supervise in hallways, in the cafeteria, at dismissal? Do you make observations in classrooms? Do you work with students in the library?

List the activities which take up most of the time in your typical day at school. List them in two different ways: how much time they are given each day with the first item listed getting more time than any other item and continue your list in descending order of time taken by each activity. Then rank them according to importance with 1 being the most important:

Activities which take up most of my time on a typical day at school, listed in order of amount of time each activity is given...

———

1.

2.

3.

4.

5.

6.

7.

8.

Ranking of those same activities in terms of importance, with 1 being the most important...

_____

1.

2.

3.

4.

5.

6.

7.

8.

Do the two lists match? Are you spending more time on the work activity which is most important than you are spending on anything else? Evaluate yourself to see if the work activities which are the highest priorities are getting the greatest amount of your time. If yes, what are you doing to make that happen? If no, what can be done to make that happen?

Yes – this is what I am doing to make that happen

———

———

No – this is what can be done to make that happen

———

What are some sources of great ideas about making improvements in what we do at school and in how we do our work at school? Teachers rarely get to see other teachers teach, yet much can be learned by observing colleagues. What works best in a Science classroom could provide ideas for what could work well in a Math, English, or Social Studies classroom. Talking to colleagues about what matters most and how they strive to allocate time so the priorities get the share of time they deserve can be very productive conversations.

Educators in a school rarely get to see other educators do their job. Is there something the librarian knows about research that he or she teaches a student in the library which a teacher could learn from and use in the classroom? Is there a discipline system that a teacher is using in the classroom which the school administrators could learn from and see if it could be applied by teachers who need guidance on classroom management?

Is there a student who is struggling in one class, but who is doing quite well in another class? Does the teacher in the class where the student is struggling know what is working best in the other classroom? Trading success stories and communicating about successful actions can be part of how a school makes sure that everyone knows what works best and knows how to do what works best.

Are there any people at the school who are frustrated because they have clearly identified what matters most, and they are confident that they have identified what works best, but things just are not going well for various reasons? Can people at the school who have figured out how to outsmart these frustrations offer guidance and encouragement to their frustrated colleagues? Yes, of course, if that kind of interaction is made a priority, and if that very useful and caring support is offered genuinely and is received properly.

The idea of trading success stories and of trading ideas about successful actions is an important reminder that much good work is being done in schools. We know what works best, and we know what matters most. Reality tells us that working in schools can be rewarding and productive, yet working in schools is challenging and can be quite difficult. With those realistic thoughts in mind, we turn to the third of our vital questions: "What makes this work so difficult, and what can I do about that reality?"

WHAT MAKES THIS WORK SO DIFFICULT, AND WHAT CAN I DO ABOUT THAT REALITY?

"As usual, lunch is the best part of a day of professional development. I know that the people who made the presentations in the morning meant well, but they just came in to present their program, get paid, and then leave at the end of the day to go make the same presentation to some other school tomorrow. I can predict that the second half of their presentation this afternoon will be every bit as bad as what they did in the morning. Both presenters admitted that they had not worked in a school for over 20 years. How could they possibly know how I should do my job? Why is this done to us?"

The very experienced teacher, Jason Clay, who offered those thoughts already knew the answer to his question. His good friend, another experienced teacher, Stephanie Madison, replied with the true, but disappointing, answer.

"Oh, it's like this most years. Somebody in some position of power decides that every person at every school in the school district or in the state has to be trained in some new teaching method or in some issue that has been making headlines. Someone is hired to come make a presentation so our school can say that we met the

mandate for training. You are right, the afternoon will be more of the same. Some people won't pay attention. Some people will try to take it seriously, but that will not be easy. We're stuck, Jason, we're just stuck."

Jason continued his venting.

"There is so much work that we need to do. The school year starts in two days. Every teacher in the building has work to do to prepare for classes and to make sure that everything is ready for the first day. I'm sure the school counselors need to be in their offices to meet with families who are arriving today to enroll students. The principal and the assistant principal need to work with the new teachers to help them prepare for their first day of teaching. This waste of time just makes everything so much more difficult. Our work is difficult enough without wasting a day right before the school year starts."

Stephanie had to agree.

"Jason, you are so right. The bad news is that lunch is over, and we have to get back to our professional development program. The good news is that in three hours this program will be over, and then we can do some work which will actually matter."

Give some emphasis to Jason's comment, "Our work is difficult enough without wasting a day right before the school year starts." Jason is right. His work as a teacher is difficult, demanding, exhausting, more complex each year, and while filled with many accomplishments, it is also filled with many frustrations and with some occasional heartbreaks.

What is difficult about working in a school? Make a list of reasons in response to that question.

1.

2.

3.

4.

5.

6.

7.

8.

9.

10.

11.

12.

13.

14.

15.

16.

Some of the items on your list may be beyond what an individual educator can do much, if anything, about. Some of the items on your list may be beyond what a school can do much, if anything, about. Let's concentrate on what we can impact directly. From the list of reasons you just wrote regarding what makes working at a school such difficult work, evaluate those in terms of what you as an individual educator and what your school as an organization can impact and then identify what can be done. This time, list only the difficulties which you and/or your school can do something effective about. Be bold, but realistic.

Difficulty	What I can do about it	What my school can do about it
1.		
2.		
3.		
4.		

Difficulty	What I can do about it	What my school can do about it
5.		
6.		
7.		
8.		

Difficulty	What I can do about it	What my school can do about it
9.		
10.		
11.		
12.		

Difficulty	What I can do about it	What my school can do about it
13.		
14.		
15.		
16.		

You will notice that there were sixteen spaces for the first list and sixteen spaces for the second list. Perhaps the two lists were identical. Yet, it is quite realistic and quite possible that your first list is longer than your second list. Why? Some problems which schools face are just beyond the reach of any one educator and any one school. That does not mean that those problems are in the impossible to solve category. Rather, it means that those problems need to be solved by other people, by other organizations, or through highly organized partnerships between educators, schools, families, other organizations, and communities.

What does make the work of being a teacher, a principal, or any other educator who works at a school so difficult? The following list may match with some of what the reader listed previously.

1. There are too many forms to fill out.
2. There are too many records to maintain and to update.
3. There are too many situations, incidents, and events which must be documented.
4. There are too many e-mails to keep up with.
5. There are too many requests for data and for data analysis.
6. Some parents or guardians never believe what we tell them about their children.
7. Some parents or guardians complain about everything.
8. Some parents or guardians threaten legal action.
9. Some students are late to school often.
10. Some students are late to class often, rarely pay attention in class, do not turn in homework, but I am responsible for their education even if they

make no effort.

11. Some students skip school.

12. There are some students who have no concern about the punishments which can be imposed on them at school.

13. Some students are bullies at school, some students steal at school, and some students disrupt school.

14. There are so many papers to grade.

15. There are too many meetings to attend.

16. The school district mandates more duties for the school each year.

17. The state government mandates more duties for schools each year.

18. The annual tests given to students do not fully or accurately measure all of the work which is done at school for students or by students, but those tests create the perceptions many people have of a school.

19. There is a lot of great work which occurs at school, but the local media give that very little attention.

20. The professional development programs we have to attend are rarely useful.

21. Every few years there is some big reform of education. We have to change everything. Then the reform does not work, and another reform follows it, but that reform also fails.

22. The discipline system at school is not strict enough.

23. Students who do behave and who do take school seriously are not given the attention and the recognition which they deserve.

24. No matter how hard I work and no matter how

great the results are that I get, the people who run this school and this school district do not acknowledge my effort.

25. Students fail my class on purpose and then get to make up the class with some computer tutorial or some other easy option. Why give them an incentive to fail a class? Why give them an easy option instead of making them do the work the first time?

26. If you are an athlete at school, you get a lot of attention. If you are a scholar at school, you get very little attention. It would help me get the best work from my students if we most acknowledged the work which school is supposed to be about: learning in the classroom.

27. Some students are addicted to their cell phones or to other electronic devices. The hours they spend each day with these devices are hours they do not spend on school work. Plus, I have to deal with their defiance in class when they intentionally and repeatedly disobey the rules about not using devices during class time.

28. Some high school students work 20 or 30 hours each week at their part-time job. Then they sleep through class, and they do no work in class.

29. We tell families how to be sure that their child is ready for kindergarten, but still many students come to kindergarten unprepared.

30. We give students reading to do over the summer. Some of them do it seriously, but others never do any of the summer reading.

31. The curriculum changes every few years in the

grade I teach or in the subject I teach. We are never told why the changes were made. The changes don't seem to be any better than what we had before, but the changes create a mountain of work to do.

32. Some students are dealing with personal issues and/or with family issues which go beyond what a teacher or a principal can resolve. What am I supposed to do?

33. I am at school for 10 hours each day. I do school work at home two hours each night. I do about 10 hours of school work each weekend. It's too much. It's just too much.

34. The school is far too crowded.

35. The copy machines break fairly often.

36. I don't have enough copies of our books to give one to each student.

37. We are told to use technology a lot. I plan lessons which will include technology and then the system does down.

38. Some students are allowed to miss many days of school for various events or activities. Those may be interesting, but it doubles my work when I have to get them caught up.

39. When a teacher of another class plans a field trip and it means some students miss my class, it creates more work for me. How does this make sense? Why is their class and their field trip more important than my class?

40. Announcements are made on the school's public address system many times during each day. Each time that happens, it interrupts the work I am doing with my students.

41. With the large number of students at this

school, we need more school counselors.

42. The principal of the school is told by the central office leaders to attend too many meetings away from school during school days.

43. The tests which are required by the state government change every few years. How can teachers know what to do if the tests which are a big part of evaluating schools keep changing?

44. The state government requires too many tests. We spend about five school days each year on tests. Plus, our school district requires more testing. All of those testing days are days which are not spent on instruction.

45. Every person who works in the school is a direct report to the principal. How can the leader of a school manage well with that many direct reports? On any given day, each person in the school could ask to meet with the principal about some issue which no other person has the authority to deal with fully.

46. There are safety measures the school needs to take, but the building was not designed with the safety needs of today in mind. How can the school leaders and other adults at school protect everyone at the school?

47. The library needs to order some new books and needs to get some new computers, but budgets for those items were reduced last year and are being reduced again this year.

48. Because the school is too crowded, each classroom is too crowded. Some classrooms have more students than there are desks in those classrooms.

49. Part of the student body at our school is a

transient population. That is just the way it is. A student might be here for a month, leave for two months, and return. Each day, there is some movement like that of students coming, going, coming back, and going again.

50. Teachers are observed only twice a year by a principal or an assistant principal. How is that enough observation time for any valid conclusions to be reached or any helpful advice to be given?

Time out. Wait a minute. The reader/co-author and the author of this book just compiled long lists of factors which indicate some of the reasons why it is so difficult to work at a school. Those lists could be added to and expanded to include more factors. Do the difficulties define and control the experience of working at a school? No, they do not, and they must not.

Be not dismayed, distressed, discouraged, or apprehensive about the many factors which make it difficult to work at a school. Rather, be determined, resolute, resilient, and confident. Know that the work which you do at your school not only can be done well, but is being done well often by many people, including you.

For reassurance and for inspiration, for guidance and for answers, think about the ideas you reflected on in chapter one and in chapter two of this book. In those chapters, our attention was on the most important goal for the school, doing what matters most, and doing what works best. Chapter three realistically addresses factors which make it difficult to work at a school. Chapters one and two provide answers for dealing with those difficulties, in truth, for mastering those difficulties so the many valuable and productive aspects of working at a school can prevail.

Persistent pursuit of the school's most important goal followed by achievement of the school's most important goal adds more to the school than all of the difficulties can take away. Dedication to always do what is right and dedication to always do what works best add more to the school than all of the difficulties can take away.

We are not faced with impossible difficulties or with an overall impossibly difficult job. We are faced with demanding work, with obstacles, and with daily challenges of our endurance. We are faced with daily situations which require total application of our ability, of our energy, and of our knowledge. We are faced with daily situations which can become opportunities to team up with colleagues so we benefit from the wisdom which can be offered by each person who works at our school.

We face daily tests of our dedication, our persistence, our commitment, and our endurance. Those tests can strengthen our dedication, our persistence, our commitment, and our endurance. We can and we must prevail.

We are also face to face with daily opportunities to favorably impact lives of students, to make a difference for good in the education of our students, to team up with colleagues, to pursue the school's most important goal, to do what matters most, and to do what works best.

It is for such honorable reasons that we chose to be educators and that education chose us to do this fascinating, complex, difficult, vital, sometimes heart-breaking, and many times inspiring work.

The acknowledgment of difficulties is surpassed by the confirmation that we know what works. We can make contributions to our school's body of knowledge about what works and to the education profession's body of knowledge about what works. With those thoughts in mind, we move to chapter four in which we will ask, "Am I always learning about my work, and am I always improving in my work?"

AM I ALWAYS LEARNING ABOUT MY WORK, AND AM I ALWAYS IMPROVING?

"I've been wondering about something. I have been a teacher for 14 years. I intend to teach for another 20 years or so. In the first few years of my teaching career, everything was new to me. I had done everything in college I needed to so I could be certified as a teacher. But being in my own classroom was really different than what I expected. I learned so much during those first few years. Actually, I learned a lot in the first few days. I had to make many changes, but it worked. I had a great mentor during my first year. The school had a super program for first year teachers, and we were matched with a mentor who was a teacher. With her help, I not only made it through the first year, but I did a good job."

Rachael Taylor's thoughts got a response from her teaching colleague, Dominique Alexander.

"Yeah, I know what you mean. That first year was tough, but I decided early in my first year that I would seek the advice of other people at the school. There were so many great teachers at the school where I worked then, just like there are here at this school. So rather than suffer in silence in my classroom after school, I went to talk to other teachers. They were great. Their advice was

brilliant. And a few of them came to observe me teach. The suggestions, the corrections, the help, and just the fact that someone cared really helped me."

Dominique smiled as she remembered those good experiences. Rachael had an idea.

"That makes me think. Everyone at this school is doing something really good each day. The teachers, the school counselors, the principal, and everyone else. We never get to see anyone else do their job, but there is so much we could all learn from each other. You and I could start. I'll visit your classroom soon and then you visit mine. The whole idea will be to learn. I'm sure you do some things with your students that I have never thought of, but that I could put to good use. I hope you can get some good ideas from seeing how I teach. When can we start?"

Rachael was energized by this idea. Dominique was equally enthusiastic.

"How about tomorrow? You have third period as planning time, so you can visit my class then. I have second period as planning time, so I could visit your class then. After school or maybe at lunch tomorrow, we could talk about everything we saw and all that we learned."

Rachael agreed.

"Great plan. Tomorrow will be a fantastic day. Thanks for doing this. Now, our short lunch time is over, and it is time to teach. Ready. Set. Go."

Cathy Weathers was exhausted. It had been a very long day at school. She arrived at 6:45 a.m., and due to several meetings after school plus 47 e-mails to deal with, she stayed at school until 6:00 p.m. She knew before becoming a principal 10 years ago that being a principal would mean long days at school, plus work to finish each night at home and each weekend at home. Her four years as an assistant principal had introduced her to much of the work of a school administrator, but being the principal meant additional duties.

There was one very important advantage she gave herself in her work as a principal: she kept in touch with the person who, years ago, had suggested that she leave her work as a teacher and become a school principal. It was good advice. Cathy still had the heart of a teacher and she did her work today with the same devotion and dedication she took into her classroom during the nine wonderful years she was a teacher. By keeping in touch with her mentor, she always had a source of good advice and of sincere encouragement.

There was another advantage that Cathy gave herself. Cathy organized an informal meeting of principals and assistant principals from her school district so Cathy and her colleagues in school administration work could share ideas, express concerns, acknowledge problems, and create solutions. She was determined to be a great principal, always. To reach that goal and to maintain that level, she needed to always learn and to always improve. Working closely with her network of colleagues was productive and was encouraging.

Cathy gave herself one more advantage. She listened to people at her school. She did not see herself as the only source of good ideas for the school. She did have decisions to make which only she could make based on the duties of her job, but she listened before making those decisions. This priority given to listening created much goodwill in the school; plus, there were many times when Cathy had an "I would never have thought of that" moment. Listening was a good way to learn and a good way to improve.

Ernesto Rodriguez worked with Cathy Weathers for three years. He served as the assistant principal of the school. With Cathy's encouragement, one year ago Ernesto applied for two local principal jobs. Ernesto was selected to be the principal of a middle school which is on the same large campus as the elementary school where he had worked with Cathy for the three years.

At the end of his first year as a principal, Ernesto thought deeply about what he had accomplished, what he had done well, what he needed to improve, and what he needed to learn. It had been a good year. His goal was for the next year to be better. In fact, his goal was for each year to be better than the year before.

During the summer after his first year as principal, Ernesto called two members of the school's faculty and staff each day to get their ideas, to hear their concerns, to ask them questions. He also called the parents and guardians of many students to see what ideas and concerns they had. Ernesto decided that he would continue this communication during his second year as principal. There was much to learn. There were many ways to improve. Hearing from colleagues and hearing from families would be an increased part of his continuous learning and continuous improvement plan.

There are many ways to learn about the work we do at

school. There are many ways to improve in the work we do at school. Let's make a list, together. The author will start the list and the reader, who is the co-author, will add to the list.

1. Read professional journals about teaching, about school counseling, about school administration, about libraries, and about other aspects of working at school.
2. Join a professional educator's group.
3. Attend conferences about education. Be selective: attend only the conferences which are known to emphasize practical, useful, realistic, and proven ideas.
4. Participate in a Professional Learning Community group at school. Be sure the group is not just another level in the school's bureaucracy, but that it is truly professionals who learn together with a sense of community.
5. Evaluate the results in your classroom. Did today's lesson work the way it was intended to work or not? If it worked, why? If not, why?
6. Take a graduate school class about education.
7. Selectively attend professional development programs. There are some professional development presentations which educators are required to attend. Attend those and do all you can to learn while you are there. When you have choices in professional development programs to attend, select those which would be most useful to you.
8. Talk to colleagues. Make the time to trade ideas with colleagues, to ask questions of colleagues, and to observe colleagues.

9. For school administrators, get out of the office as much as possible. More will be learned by frequent interaction with people than by being in the office. Of course, some office work is required, but working directly with people in every part of the school is more important.

10. Read good books about education. Re-read the best books you read about education when you were in college or in graduate school. Have your ideas changed any since you originally read those books? Do the books speak to you now as they did then?

11. If there is a particular topic you would like to learn about, ask the librarian(s) at your school for resources about that topic.

12. Meet with people who work with your school district's central office. Their years of experience are filled with lessons learned that can be shared with you.

13. Attend a school board meeting in your school district to keep up with current issues and with emerging issues.

14. Contact people who taught you. Gain insights from their experience. Contact people who were a school counselor, an assistant principal, or the principal at schools you attended. Gain from their perspectives and insights.

15. Read some current materials about the subjects you teach. Keep learning about the subjects you teach and about new knowledge in the subjects.

16. For school administrators, read leadership and management books which are not designed for principals. Some of the best writing about leadership and management is done for business executives, so get the benefits of that knowledge.

17. Make faculty meetings a time to share great teaching ideas and great teaching methods.
18. For school administrators, talk with people in your community who have leadership and management duties in organizations other than schools. Learn from them and learn with them. Build partnerships with them that could benefit your school and which could benefit their organization.
19. For school counselors, keep in touch with people who do counseling work in settings other than schools. Learn from them and learn with them. Build partnerships with them which could benefit your school and which could benefit their organizations.
20. Think. Reflect. Ponder. At the end of each school day, think about what worked well; what was acceptable, but could have been better; what did not work; what unexpected difficulties emerged and how can such situations be prevented or minimized in the future; what unexpected opportunities came up and what can be done to create the possibility of more of those.

21.

22.

23.

24.

25.

26.

27.

28.

29.

30.

31.

32.

33.

34.

35.

36.

37.

38.

39.

40.

Victor Livingston always liked his name, a lot. He associated his first name with the word victory. When he combined victory with part of his last name—living—he decided that his name told him that throughout his life he could, with the right work ethic, have many victories. He knew that there could be and would be some defeats or some disappointments, but he intended to live victoriously. His name demanded that, and his name inspired that.

Victor became a high school math teacher and intended for all students in each of his classes to have academic victories by learning all there was to learn, by making good grades, by realizing how important it is to work and think, and by behaving properly.

Victor got good results as a teacher. He put in the extra time and effort it takes to do superior work. He attended worthwhile education conferences in the summers and he selected useful professional development programs to attend during each school year. He worked closely with the other teachers in his math department.

During his first few years of teaching, Victor kept noticing that some of his students were dealing with serious issues. A few of his students had been court involved. One student was expelled from school. Several students were suspended from school, repeatedly. Victor did have many students who took school seriously, were conscientious about their work, and who were polite. Still, he had not expected to encounter such serious and severe issues with a sizable number of students.

When Victor decided to go to graduate school, he designed his program so he would become certified as a school counselor. Victor had always liked Math and he was a very effective Math teacher, but he found himself thinking more and more about problems that some students faced and those problems he was thinking about were not Math problems. They were people problems.

During each year as a teacher, Victor had spent much time talking with the school counselors at the high school where he taught. He also met occasionally with behavioral specialists and a social worker who worked in his school district's central office. He needed to learn if there were any ways that he could assist the students who were so troubled. He also was attending graduate school part-time in addition to full-time teaching. His emphasis in graduate school was to become a school counselor.

When Victor completed his graduate school work and earned certification as a school counselor, he searched for school counseling jobs. After two years of searching and of interviewing, Victor was selected to be a high school counselor at the school where he had been a teacher. This decision was made as a school year ended. Victor knew that he would miss the classroom, but he also knew that he had a new opportunity to teach in a different way. He was thrilled about the possibilities of what he could accomplish as a school counselor. He also realized that there was much he did not know.

Victor asked the other counselors at his school if they could meet with him occasionally during the summer before the school year began. They agreed and that began a series of weekly meetings. Victor said he learned as much from those meetings as he did from some of his graduate school classes.

Victor asked his school counselor colleagues if

they could continue to meet throughout the school year. The answer was yes. Victor knew that he could be a good school counselor. He also knew that by getting words of wisdom from experienced and well-respected colleagues, he could become a great counselor.

Taking into account all of the ideas and case studies in this chapter, the reader/co-author has four questions to think about and to write about as we conclude chapter four.

What am I doing to always learn more about my work?

_____

1.

2.

3.

4.

5.

6.

7.

8.

9.

10.

What else could I do to learn more about my work?

———

1.

2.

3.

4.

5.

What am I doing to always improve in my work?

_____

1.

2.

3.

4.

5.

6.

7.

8.

9.

10.

What else could I do to improve in my work?
_____

1.

2.

3.

4.

5.

Congratulations. You have seriously thought about and deeply reflected upon the four vital questions for teachers and principals. You added to this book with your writing, your ideas, your perspective, your hopes, your frustrations, your lessons learned, your experiences and your plans. We move now to some concluding thoughts for this book, yet there is every reason to continue the thinking and the learning which this book has been a catalyst for.

Re-read this book occasionally. On a given day, a particular page or a certain chapter could be just what you need as a source of guidance, of insight, of inspiration, and of ideas. Read, read more, keep reading. Think, think more, keep thinking. Teach, teach more, keep teaching. Lead, lead more, keep leading. Believe, commit, persist, prevail.

EPILOGUE: BELIEVE, COMMIT, PERSIST, PREVAIL

Long before there were four vital questions for teachers and principals, there have been four vital virtues for anyone who would become an educator. Those virtues are belief in education, commitment to education, persistence so learning is caused, and prevailing in the responsibilities of an educator who endures the difficulties in order to create successes.

Belief in education means you truly believe that education is important, that proper educational experiences can be provided so each student learns, and that wholesome education enhances the quality of life.

Making a commitment to education means that you have selected this career because being an educator is a significant part of who you are and is, therefore, what you must do. You commit daily to your students, your school, your profession, and to your conscience, which tells you when you are doing the job well and when you need to do the job better.

To persist is to work and push through the difficulties which are certain to come. To persist is to put in the extra time each day that separates below average, average, good, and great. You are committed to and you persist toward the level of greatness in your work. You are satisfied with nothing less because greatness is within reach. You stretch yourself so greatness is reached.

To prevail is to be the teacher you promised yourself you would be when you chose education as a career and when education chose you to be part of the grand adventure of causing learning to happen in the mind of each student. To prevail is to live up to the promises you made yourself when you became a school counselor, a librarian, an assistant principal, a principal, an academic dean, a dean of students, or any other position which during your career became a way for you to be of service to the cause of education.

When the four virtues of an authentic educator—believe, commit, persist, prevail—are combined with true, bold, practical, and inspiring answers to the four vital questions for teachers and principals, the results are unlimited, purposeful, important, and rewarding. They can be exhausting to achieve, punctuated with difficulties, yet are very meaningful. The conclusion is to believe, to commit, to persist, and to prevail. One way to help do that is to think, think more, and keep thinking about the four vital questions for teachers and principals.

ACKNOWLEDGMENTS

My deepest thanks go to my family, past and present. My parents, Bob and Judy Babbage, made education a very high priority in our home. With their support, my educational experiences as a student were filled with much learning and with many accomplishments.

My grandparents, Keen and Eunice Johnson, confirmed that education was a very high priority in our family. They often encouraged me when I began thinking about becoming a teacher. Their help was essential.

My brother and sister-in-law, Bob and Laura Babbage, along with my nephews, Robert and Brian, plus my niece, Julie, have given me guidance, advice, and encouragement in my career as an educator and in my endeavors as an author. I cherish our bond.

Adam Turner is an absolute superstar in the work of turning a manuscript into a book. My job is to write the words, the pages, the chapters. His job is to turn that material into a book. He always designs covers which capture the essence of the book. His skills are superior.

I was a student in the Fayette County (Kentucky) Public Schools for 12 years from 1960-1972 during my time in elementary school, middle school, and high school. I was taught by outstanding teachers and led by outstanding school administrators. It was my good fortune to work for that same school district for 23 years from 1993-2016. Those were great years. I am thankful for those experiences.

During 1989-1993, I was a doctoral student in the University of Kentucky's College of Education. That program provided everything I could ask for and more. It was more work than I imagined it would be. It was more beneficial than I thought possible.

ABOUT THE AUTHOR

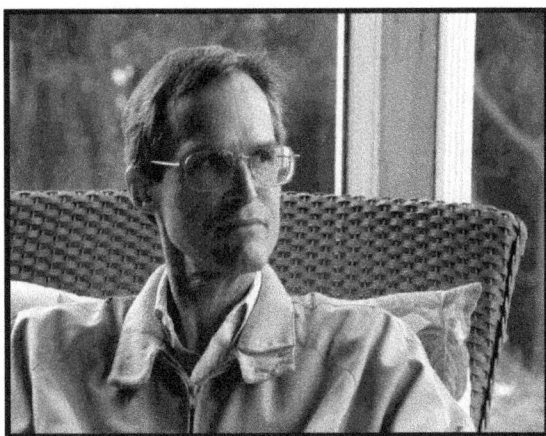

Keen Babbage, Ed. D., retired from a 27-year career in public education in 2016. He had been a middle school teacher, a middle school assistant principal, and a high school teacher. Earlier and later in his career, he worked for seven years at three private schools. He has also worked in advertising/marketing for eight years at three large companies.

He has written 20 books about education with emphasis on two areas: teaching, and school leadership/management. He has written three additional books: *Life Lessons from Cancer* (co-authored by Laura Babbage); *Life Lessons from a Dog Named Rudy*; and *Take More Naps*. He lives in Lexington, Kentucky.

www.ingramcontent.com/pod-product-compliance
Lightning Source LLC
Chambersburg PA
CBHW022009090426
42741CB00007B/952